FOR SADIE, MY
FAVORITE FELINE.

Published by Familius LLC, www.familius.com

Familius books are available at special discounts for bulk purchases for sales
promotions or for family or corporate use. Special editions, including personalized
covers, excerpts of existing books, or books with corporate logos, can be created in
large quantities for special needs. For more information, contact Premium Sales at
559-876-2170 or email specialmarkets@familius.com.

Library of Congress Catalog-in-Publication Data
2015942357
ISBN 9781942672968

Edited by Liza Hagerman
Jacket and book design by David Miles
Photography credits: Shutterstock.com

10 9 8 7 6 5 4 3 2 1

First Edition
Printed in China

BROOKE
JORDEN

IF IT FITS, I SITS

THE ULTIMATE CAT QUOTEBOOK

FAMILIUS

CONTENTS

· ·

CAT LOGIC:
AN INTRODUCTION

A caveat before I begin:

> THERE IS, INCIDENTALLY, NO WAY OF
> TALKING ABOUT CATS THAT ENABLES ONE
> TO COME OFF AS A SANE PERSON.
>
> —DAN GREENBERG

I accept this now, and I think I know why.

I haven't always been a cat person. My family owned various pets—dogs, rabbits, turtles, lizards—but my father firmly insisted that we would never own a cat. Cats, he preached, are evil. And so, I laughed when peasants used cats to beat rugs (*Monty Python and the Holy Grail*) and when Jerry dropped [insert a heavy object] on top of poor Tom.

Years went by this way. I grew up, got married, bought a house, and then, one day, something changed. In a moment of clarity, I announced to my husband, "Let's get a cat." We adopted a beautiful orange tabby from the shelter near our home, and almost immediately, I was converted. Cats are so clean, so quiet, so graceful, and so deliciously curious—except for when they are whiny, clumsy, and unbelievably lazy. These intense oppositions crammed into such a small, furry body are fascinating.

I thought surely I would begin to understand our little Sadie with time; she was my first cat, I reasoned. And yes, with time, I grew accustomed to her odd habits and her particular needs, but I still never understood the whys behind them, and I'm not sure I ever will. Why does she stare at the walls as if she can see through them? Why does she insist upon drinking from the sink instead of her water dish? Why does she prefer the cardboard box to the wonderful toys that came in it?

Cats are just animals, some people may insist. That's all there is to it.

Maybe I'm crazy, but I suspect there must be so much more brewing behind those luminous eyes. The privilege of every cat lover—from artists and philosophers to crazy old "cat ladies"—is to wonder at the puzzle that is cat logic. As Carole Wilbourn put it:

"The constant challenge to decipher feline behavior is perhaps one of the most fascinating qualities of owning a cat."

CARDBOARD BOXES

CATS AND THEIR PECULIARITIES

Cats are persnickety. They tend to like things just so, and anything that throws off the status quo earns a piercingly silent glare. Cat owners can, eventually, understand their cat's habits and needs. More perplexing, though—and more entertaining—are the peculiarities that have nothing to do with habit or survival and everything to do with being a cat.

Cats can be impatient: "I think you should wake up and feed me NOW."

Cats can be indecisive: "The door's open, but should I stay inside or go outside . . . or inside . . . or outside?"

Cats can be stubborn: "I know you are calling me, but I'm going to take my sweet time about coming . . . and only because you might have food."

Cats can be particular: "I want you to rub my tummy, but only twice. And only with one hand. And only on my left side."

Like I said . . . persnickety. But we love them, anyway.

IT IS REMARKABLE, IN CATS, THAT THE OUTER LIFE THEY REVEAL TO THEIR MASTERS IS ONE OF PERPETUAL

BOREDOM.

—Robley Wilson Jr.

THERE IS NO SNOOZE BUTTON ON A CAT WHO WANTS BREAKFAST.

—Anonymous

A CAT IS A PUZZLE FOR WHICH THERE IS NO SOLUTION.

—Hazel Nicholson

EVERY
THING
COMES TO
THOSE WHO
WAIT...

EXCEPT A CAT.

—Mario Andretti

THE MATHEMATICAL
PROBABILITY OF A
COMMON CAT
DOING EXACTLY AS IT PLEASES
IS THE ONE SCIENTIFIC
ABSOLUTE
IN THE WORLD.

—Lynn M. Osband

MEOW

IS LIKE ALOHA—
IT CAN MEAN
ANYTHING.

—HANK KETCHAM

MOST BEDS

SLEEP UP TO SIX CATS.

TEN CATS

WITHOUT THE OWNER.

—STEPHEN BAKER

FOR A MAN TO
TRULY UNDERSTAND
REJECTION,
HE MUST FIRST
BE IGNORED BY
A CAT.

—Anonymous

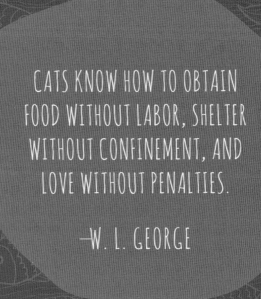

CATS KNOW HOW TO OBTAIN
FOOD WITHOUT LABOR, SHELTER
WITHOUT CONFINEMENT, AND
LOVE WITHOUT PENALTIES.

—W. L. GEORGE

CATS

CAN BE COOPERATIVE WHEN
SOMETHING FEELS GOOD, WHICH, TO
A CAT, IS THE WAY EVERYTHING IS
SUPPOSED TO FEEL AS MUCH OF THE
TIME AS POSSIBLE.

—ROGER CARAS

CATS

ARE RATHER DELICATE
CREATURES AND THEY ARE
SUBJECT TO A GOOD MANY
AILMENTS, BUT I NEVER HEARD
OF ONE WHO SUFFERED FROM
INSOMNIA.

—Joseph Wood Krutch

ANYTHING NOT
NAILED DOWN IS A

CAT
TOY.

—ANONYMOUS

THE REAL MEASURE OF A
DAY'S HEAT IS THE LENGTH
OF A SLEEPING CAT.

—CHARLES J. BRADY

MOST CATS,
WHEN THEY ARE
OUT
WANT TO BE IN,
AND VICE VERSA,
AND OFTEN SIMULTANEOUSLY.

—Louis J. Camuti

ANYONE WHO CONSiDERS PROTOCOL UNIMPORTANT HAS NEVER DEALT WITH A CAT.

—Robert A. Heinlein

CHAPTER 2

ENEMY #1

CATS AND DOGS

Most people would tell you that a dog is the opposite of a cat. They are, after all, very different creatures in terms of temperament, habit, volume, and hygiene. Dogs are lovable in their ignorance, while cats are mystifying in their discretion.

To my mind, dogs are like human babies, while cats are more like human teenagers. Dogs are innocent, a bit clueless, needy, and unfailingly loving. Like infants, they look to their owners for every need, from food to affection.

Cats, on the other hand, resemble typical human teens. They take pride in their independence (despite the fact that their owners care for and feed them), and so they tend to be a tad ungrateful. They always seem to have an "attitude"—and oh, the drama! They are masters of the silent treatment. They may, in a matter of minutes, display both great wisdom and maturity and utter silliness or infantile whining. And yet, when cats show those glimmers of vulnerability and affection, we melt. Those moments mean so much more because they are not a given; they are a luxury.

But we still wouldn't give them the car keys.

DOGS EAT.
CATS DINE.

—Ann Taylor

THE DIFFERENCE BETWEEN DOGS AND CATS IS THAT A DOG WILL RESPOND BUT A CAT WILL TAKE A MESSAGE AND GET BACK TO YOU.

—MARY BLY

CATS ARE
SMARTER
THAN DOGS.
YOU CAN'T
GET EIGHT
CATS TO
PULL A SLED
THROUGH
SNOW.

—Jeff Valdez

Cats are the ultimate narcissists. You can tell this by all the time they spend on personal grooming. Dogs aren't like this. A dog's idea of personal grooming is to roll in a dead fish.

–James Gorman

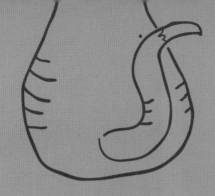

WOMEN AND CATS WILL
DO AS THEY PLEASE, AND
MEN AND DOGS SHOULD
RELAX AND GET USED
TO THE IDEA.

—ANONYMOUS

IF ANIMALS COULD SPEAK, THE DOG WOULD BE A BLUNDERING, OUTSPOKEN FELLOW, BUT THE CAT WOULD HAVE THE RARE GRACE OF NEVER SAYING A WORD TOO MUCH.

—MARK TWAIN

DOGS HAVE MASTERS. CATS HAVE STAFF.

—ANONYMOUS

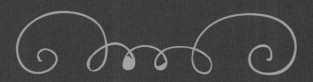

If a dog jumps in your lap, it is because he is fond of you; but if a cat does the same thing, it is because your lap is warmer.

—Alfred North Whitehead

DOGS
ARE like KIDS.
CATS
ARE like
ROOM
MATES.

—Oliver Gaspirtz, *A Treasury of Pet Humor*

A DOG KNOWS HIS MASTER; A CAT DOES NOT.

—Eleazar B. Zadok

CHAPTER 3

BREAK OUT THE LINT ROLLER

CATS AND CAT LOVERS

Cat lovers are in on a secret. There is nothing so interesting as a cat, nothing so delightful as hearing it purr, and nothing so gratifying as winning its heart. And did I mention purring? Don't even get me started on the cuteness of purring.

Our house plants may be shredded, our black pants may be covered in hair, and our laps may be permanently spoken for, but we don't mind; in fact, we love it. We love our cats.

Let the haters call us crazy, but we cat lovers know the truth—cats make the best pets.

I simply can't resist a cat, particularly a purring one. They are the cleanest, cunningest, and most intelligent things I know—outside of the girl you love, of course.

—Mark Twain, *Abroad with Mark Twain and Eugene Field*, Henry Fisher

YOU HAVEN'T LIVED UNTIL YOU'VE LIVED WITH A CAT.

—Doris Day

I LOVE CATS
BECAUSE I ENJOY
MY HOME, AND
LITTLE BY LITTLE,
THEY BECOME
ITS VISIBLE
SOUL.

—Jean Cocteau

WHAT GREATER
GIFT THAN THE
LOVE
OF A CAT?

—Charles Dickens

CAT LOVERS TURN INTO
CAT COLLECTORS.

–GREG KINNEAR

CAT PEOPLE

ARE DIFFERENT TO THE
EXTENT THAT THEY
GENERALLY ARE NOT
CONFORMISTS. HOW COULD
THEY BE WITH A CAT
RUNNING THEIR LIVES?

—LOUIS J. CAMUTI

THERE ARE FEW
THINGS IN LIFE MORE
HEARTWARMING
THAN TO BE
WELCOMED
BY A CAT.

—TAY HOHOFF

HOW YOU BEHAVE TOWARD CATS HERE
BELOW DETERMINES YOUR STATUS IN

HEAVEN.

—Robert A. Heinlein

THE MORE PEOPLE I MEET, THE MORE i LiKE MY CAT.

—ANONYMOUS

CHAPTER 4

SMELLY CAT

CATS AND DOG PEOPLE

Why is it that cat lovers can still like dogs, but dog people seem completely convinced that cats are soulless, hairball-emitting demons? Is there no middle ground? Why are cats so polarizing?

Perhaps there is something fundamentally different about cat and dog people. Maybe dog people prefer a pet who wears its emotions on its "sleeve" while cat people prefer a riddle, an enigma. Maybe dog people crave energetic loyalty while cat people need quiet companionship. Or maybe it can be summed up in a single word:

Allergies.

Whatever the cause, according to veterinarian Deborah A. Edwards, this tragic schism has but one explanation: "People who don't like cats just haven't met the right one yet."

PEOPLE WHO
HATE CATS
WILL COME BACK
AS MICE
IN THEIR NEXT LIFE.

—FAITH RESNICK

BEWARE OF PEOPLE WHO DISLIKE CATS.

—IRISH PROVERB

CATS AREN'T CLEAN;

THEY'RE JUST COVERED WITH CAT SPIT.

—John S. Nichols

LETTIN' THE CAT
OUTTA THE BAG
IS A WHOLE LOT
EASIER THAN PUTTIN'
IT BACK IN.

—WILL ROGERS

CATS ARE A WASTE OF FUR.

—RITA RUDNER

Dogs will give you unconditional love until the day they die. Cats will make you pay for every mistake you've ever made since the day you were born.

—Oliver Gaspirtz, *A Treasury of Pet Humor*

A DOG IS
A MAN'S
BEST
FRIEND.
A CAT IS
A CAT'S
BEST
FRIEND.

—Robert J. Vogel

CHAPTER 5

HERE, KITTY, KITTY

CATS AND THEIR "MASTERS"

When you decide to adopt a cat, what you've really done is sign a binding contract, agreeing to submit your will, your time, and your treats to the feline ruler who has entered your home. Your cat now owns you, and it will be happy to remind you of that fact if you ever happen to forget.

After all, everyone knows that "meow" is really a command to "Let ME-OUT!"

CATS WERE PUT INTO THE WORLD TO DISPROVE THE DOGMA THAT ALL THINGS WERE CREATED TO SERVE MAN.

—PAUL GRAY

AS WE ALL KNOW,

CATS NOW RULE THE WORLD.

—John R. F. Breen

CATS' HEARING APPARATUS IS
BUILT TO ALLOW THE HUMAN
VOICE TO EASILY GO IN ONE EAR
AND OUT THE OTHER.

—STEPHEN BAKER

THE CAT IS DOMESTIC ONLY AS FAR AS SUITS ITS OWN ENDS.

—Saki (H. H. Munro)

WHEN A CAT
ADOPTS YOU,
THERE IS NOTHING
TO BE DONE ABOUT
IT EXCEPT TO
PUT UP
WITH IT UNTIL
THE WIND CHANGES.

—T. S. ELIOT

CATS ARE
KINDLY MASTERS . . .

. . . JUST SO LONG
AS YOU REMEMBER
YOUR PLACE. —PAUL GRAY

There are many intelligent species in the universe.

THEY ARE ALL OWNED BY CATS.

—Anonymous

THE PHRASE DOMESTIC CAT IS AN OXYMORON.

—George F. Will

After scolding one's cat, one looks into its face and is seized by the ugly suspicion that it understood every word—and has filed it for reference.

—Charlotte Gray

CHAPTER 6

CAT'S CRADLE

CATS AND KITTENS

L et's be honest: is there anything cuter than a kitten? With their big eyes, furry bodies, and insatiable curiosity, kittens are by far the most irresistible creatures on the planet. Part of what makes them so adorable is their adventurous, uninhibited spirit. They openly show affection. They question everything. They fear nothing—except very loud noises.

Cats and humans actually follow a very similar maturation pattern. When we are young, we are fearless. We are open and curious and naïve, but we are blissful in our ignorance—we are kittens. The older we get, the more cautious we become. We reserve our emotions. We observe before we act. We are wiser, but we are also a little sadder—we are cats.

KITTENS ARE BORN WITH THEIR EYES SHUT. THEY OPEN THEM IN ABOUT SIX DAYS, TAKE A LOOK AROUND, THEN CLOSE THEM AGAIN FOR THE BETTER PART OF THEIR LIVES.

—STEPHEN BAKER

THERE IS NO MORE
INTREPID
EXPLORER
THAN A
KITTEN.

—CHAMPFLEURY

IT IS IMPOSSIBLE TO KEEP A STRAIGHT FACE

IN THE PRESENCE OF ONE OR MORE KITTENS.

—Cynthia E. Varnado

It is a very inconvenient habit of kittens (Alice had once made the remark) that whatever you say to them, they always purr.

—Lewis Carroll, *Through the Looking-Glass, and What Alice Found There*

IF ONLY CATS GREW INTO KITTENS.

—R.D. Stern

A KITTEN IS, IN THE ANIMAL WORLD, WHAT A ROSEBUD IS IN THE GARDEN.

—Robert Sowthey

ONE CAT
JUST LEADS
TO ANOTHER.

—Ernest Hemingway

CHAPTER 7

TO PURR OR NOT TO PURR

CATS AND ARTISTS, PHILOSOPHERS, AND GODS

Creative, intellectual people have always been inexplicably drawn to cats. Ernest Hemingway owned more than thirty cats in his lifetime. Perhaps such artists admire the cat's natural aesthetic beauty and innate wisdom. The cat's silence and grace make it an excellent companion for writers, artists, and philosophers of all kinds.

Or maybe there is a simpler explanation. Maybe cats see themselves as philosophers, as works of art, even as gods. And maybe similarly pretentious, romantic humans are more than happy to play along. As they say, birds of a feather . . .

In nine lifetimes, you'll never know as much about your cat as your cat knows about you.

—Michel de Montaigne

THE CAT'S FUNCTION IS TO SIT AND BE ADMIRED.

-Georgina Strickland Gates

THERE ARE TWO MEANS OF REFUGE FROM THE MISERY OF LIFE: MUSIC AND CATS.

—Albert Schweitzer

TWO THINGS ARE AESTHETICALLY PERFECT IN THE WORLD:

THE CLOCK AND THE CAT.

-Émile-Auguste Chartier

AUTHORS LIKE CATS

BECAUSE THEY ARE SUCH QUIET, LOVABLE, WISE CREATURES, AND CATS LIKE AUTHORS FOR THE SAME REASONS.

—ROBERTSON DAVIES

TIME SPENT WITH CATS IS NEVER WASTED.

—Sigmund Freud

COULD THE PURR BE ANYTHING BUT CONTEMPLATIVE?

—IRVING TOWNSEND

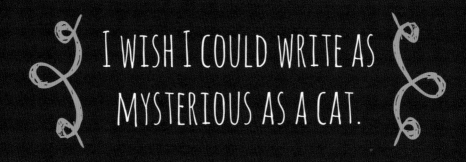

I wish I could write as mysterious as a cat.

—Edgar Allan Poe

IT ALWAYS GIVES
ME A SHIVER
WHEN i SEE
A CAT SEEING
WHAT i CAN'T SEE.

—Eleanor Farjeon

IN ANCIENT TIMES, CATS WERE WORSHIPPED AS GODS; THEY HAVE NEVER FORGOTTEN THIS.

—Terry Pratchett

IN THE BEGINNING, GOD CREATED MAN, BUT SEEING HIM SO FEEBLE, HE GAVE HIM THE CAT.

-WARREN ECKSTEIN

WHO CAN BELIEVE THAT THERE IS NO SOUL BEHIND THOSE LUMINOUS EYES?

—Théophile Gautier

I'VE MET MANY THINKERS AND MANY CATS, BUT THE WISDOM OF CATS IS INFINITELY SUPERIOR.

—Hippolyte Taine

CHAPTER 8

OF MICE AND MEN

CATS AND THEIR HUMAN QUALITIES

Since cats can be so quiet, so withdrawn, cat owners often find themselves wondering, *What are they thinking about?* We tend to anthropomorphize—to attribute human emotion to their intelligent eyes, their dignified bearing, and their knowing glances.

Cats, in their feline wisdom, represent both the best and worst of humanity—though perhaps more gracefully. They are proud, but they are loyal. They demonstrate both complete contentment and utter rage. They may be sycophants, but they are independent. They are unpredictable, and yet, most of the time, we are certain we know exactly what they are thinking.

Cats must be people, too.

WAY DOWN DEEP, WE'RE ALL MOTIVATED BY THE SAME URGES. CATS HAVE THE COURAGE TO LIVE BY THEM.

—Jim Davis

There is, indeed, no single quality of the cat that man could not emulate to his advantage.

—Carl Van Vechten

CATS INVENTED SELF-ESTEEM; THERE IS NOT AN INSECURE BONE IN THEIR BODY.

—ERMA BOMBECK

IF CATS COULD TALK, THEY WOULDN'T.

—Nan Porter

WITH THE QUALITIES OF
CLEANLINESS, AFFECTION,
PATIENCE, DIGNITY, AND
COURAGE THAT CATS HAVE, HOW
MANY OF US, I ASK YOU, WOULD
BE CAPABLE OF BECOMING CATS?

—Fernand Méry

ABOUT THE AUTHOR

Brooke Jorden is a converted cat lover. Brooke earned a BA in English and editing from Brigham Young University. Academically, Brooke's studies focused on film adaptation and fairy tales, and she presented her research most recently at the 2013 PCA/ACA National Conference in Washington, DC. Brooke previously wrote for *Stowaway*, a travel magazine, and worked on staff as an editor and senior designer. The author of *The Quotable Mom* and *The Quotable Dad*, Brooke is now a managing editor at Familius. Brooke is also a licensed Zumba® Fitness instructor, teaching several classes a week. The oldest of seven children and a believer in the importance of family, Brooke is proud to be a part of the Familius family and a proponent of its mission. She currently lives in Utah with her husband, Tyler, and their adorable cat, Sadie.

ABOUT FAMILIUS

Welcome to a place where parents are celebrated, not compared. Where heart is at the center of our families, and family is at the center of our homes. Where boo-boos are still kissed, cake beaters are still licked, and mistakes are still okay. Welcome to a place where books—and family—are beautiful. Familius: a book publisher dedicated to helping families be happy.

Website: www.familius.com
Facebook: www.facebook.com/paterfamilius
Twitter: @familiustalk, @paterfamilius1
Pinterest: www.pinterest.com/familius